The Believer's Pace- Tools for Running Life's Marathon

Joshua Rhoades

Published by Joshua Paul Rhoades, 2024.

While every precaution has been taken in the preparation of this book, the publisher assumes no responsibility for errors or omissions, or for damages resulting from the use of the information contained herein.

THE BELIEVER'S PACE- TOOLS FOR RUNNING LIFE'S MARATHON

First edition. August 26, 2024.

ISBN: 979-8224368730

Written by Joshua Rhoades.

Also by Joshua Rhoades

Courage Under Fire: David's Stand On The Battlefield
Jonah's Journey: Voices Of Redemption And Lessons In Obedience
The Furnace Of Faith: 12 Principles From The Heat Of Faith
Whispers of Hope: Inspiring Stories of Men's Prayers In Scripture
Frontier Legends: The Oregon Dream
Elijah: A Beacon Of Boldness
HOOK, LINE & SAVIOUR - Faith Reflections from Fishing
Driven By Faith: Motor Racing Inspired Christian Life
30 Day Devotional - Bold and Strong- Coffee Devotions for a
Courageous Christian Walk
Authentic Christianity: The Heart of Old Time Religion
Consider The Ant - God's Tiny Preachers
Flee Fornication: The Plea For Purity
Renewed Hope- How to Find Encouragement in God
Sounding The Call - The Voice of Conviction
The Altar - Where Heaven Meets Earth
The Bible's Battlefields- Timeless Lessons from Ancient Wars
The Sacred Art of Silence - How Silence Speaks in Scripture
Under Fire- The Sanctity of the Traditional Biblical Home
Who Is on the Lord's Side? A Call to Righteousness
What Is Truth? - From Skepticism to Submission
From Dugout to Devotion- Spiritual Lessons from Baseball
Par for the Course- Faith and Fairways
The Believer's Pace- Tools for Running Life's Marathon
The Immutable Fortress- Security in God's Unchanging Nature

Introduction

Introduction

In the grand marathon of life, every step counts, every stride matters, and every believer is called to run with purpose and perseverance. Inspired by the timeless wisdom of Hebrews 12:1-2, "The Believer's Pace: Tools for Running Life's Marathon" invites readers on a transformative journey of faith and endurance. This book is not merely a theoretical discourse on Christian living; it's a practical guide filled with actionable insights and invaluable tools to equip believers for the race set before them. Drawing upon the rich tapestry of Biblical truth and real-life experiences, each chapter of " The Believer's Pace: Tools for Running Life's Marathon " unpacks essential principles for navigating life's challenges, cultivating spiritual resilience, and finishing the race strong. From endurance and stamina to pace control and self-discipline, readers will discover a treasure trove of practical wisdom and actionable strategies to apply in their daily lives. Grounded in the enduring truths of Scripture and illuminated by the indwelling Spirit, this book offers a roadmap for running life's marathon with faith, perseverance, and grace. As readers embark on this transformative journey, may they be inspired, encouraged, and empowered to run their race with endurance, keeping their eyes "Looking unto Jesus the author and finisher of our faith".

Endurance

In 1992, during the Barcelona Olympics, one of the most remarkable displays of endurance occurred in the men's 400meter race, featuring British athlete Derek Redmond. As Redmond sprinted around the track, pushing his body to its limits, disaster struck midway through the race when he suddenly collapsed to the ground with a torn hamstring. In excruciating pain and unable to continue, Redmond's Olympic dreams seemed shattered as medical personnel rushed onto the track to assist him. However, in a moment of sheer determination and against all odds, Redmond made the decision to finish the race. With tears streaming down his face and his leg heavily bandaged, he rose to his feet and began hobbling towards the finish line, determined to complete the race he had trained so hard for. As Redmond struggled to put one foot in front of the other, his father, Jim Redmond, broke through security barriers and ran onto the track to support his son. Together, they made their way towards the finish line, with Jim providing a shoulder for Derek to lean on as they crossed the finish line together, to a standing ovation from the crowd. Although Derek Redmond did not win a medal that day, his display of courage, resilience, and unwavering determination captured the hearts of millions around the world and remains one of the most memorable moments in Olympic history. His story serves as a powerful reminder that true victory is not always measured by medals or records, but by the strength of character and the willingness to persevere in the face of adversity.

Endurance is a multifaceted concept encompassing the ability to withstand hardship, persevere through challenges, and maintain steadfastness in pursuit of a goal. It embodies mental fortitude, physical stamina, and spiritual resilience. In its essence, endurance is the capacity to persist with patience and determination despite obstacles or adversity. Drawing from the King James Version of Hebrews 12:1-2, which admonishes believers to "run with patience the race that is set before us," endurance finds profound resonance in the Christian journey. The metaphorical imagery of a race underscores the Christian life as a journey fraught with trials, uncertainties, and spiritual battles. Just as athletes endure rigorous training and compete with unwavering determination, Christians are called to navigate the course of life with patience and perseverance. The phrase "run with patience" implies a deliberate pace, emphasizing the importance of steady progress rather than hasty sprinting. It speaks to the virtue of patience—a quality often undervalued in today's fast-paced world but essential for enduring trials and tribulations. The race "set before us" suggests a divine appointment, wherein each believer has a unique path marked out by God. This race may encompass various challenges, including persecution, temptation, doubt, and adversity, yet the call to endurance remains constant.

Practical applications of endurance in the life of a Christian involve cultivating spiritual disciplines, nurturing faith, and embracing a mindset of perseverance. Firstly, endurance entails steadfast devotion to prayer, scripture study, and communion with God, anchoring one's faith in times of uncertainty (Romans 15:4). Daily engagement with the Word of God provides sustenance for the journey, fortifying believers with spiritual nourishment and guidance (2 Timothy 3:16-17). Secondly, endurance is manifested through resilience in adversity, trusting in God's sovereignty and providence amidst trials (Romans 5:3-4). Rather than succumbing to despair or doubt, Christians are called to persevere in faith, knowing that God works all things for good to those who love Him (Romans 8:28). Thirdly, endurance involves bearing one another's burdens and supporting fellow believers in their own race of faith (Galatians 6:2). Encouragement, accountability, and fellowship within the body of Christ bolster endurance and unity amid life's challenges (Hebrews 10:24-25).

Moreover, endurance extends beyond personal struggles to encompass societal injustices, global crises, and missions of compassion and justice. By embodying Christ-like love and perseverance, Christians serve as beacons of hope and agents of transformation in a world marred by brokenness and despair. Ultimately, the call to "run with patience the race that is set before us" beckons believers to fix their eyes on Jesus, the author, and perfecter of faith (Hebrews 12:2). He exemplifies supreme endurance, enduring the cross and despising its shame for the joy set before Him (Philippians 2:8). In Christ, believers find the ultimate source of strength, perseverance, and hope (Philippians 4:13). Thus, the Christian life is not merely a sprint but a marathon—a journey of faith marked by endurance, perseverance, and unwavering trust in the promises of God. As believers press on with patience, they are assured of the crown of life awaiting those who finish the race victoriously (James 1:12).

Stamina

One of the most inspiring displays of stamina in a race comes from the 1995 Ironman World Championship held in Kona, Hawaii. The story centers around Sian Welch and Wendy Ingraham, two triathletes competing in one of the most grueling endurance events in the world. As the race entered its final leg, the marathon, both Welch and Ingraham found themselves neck and neck, vying for a podium finish. With just a few hundred meters left to go, exhaustion began to take its toll on both athletes. In a remarkable show of determination and grit, Welch and Ingraham pushed their bodies to the absolute limit, refusing to give up despite the intense physical and mental fatigue. As they approached the finish line, their bodies battered and depleted, they both stumbled and collapsed just meters away from the end. In a remarkable display of sportsmanship, instead of capitalizing on their rivals' misfortune, Welch and Ingraham extended their hands to each other and made the decision to finish the race together, crossing the finish line hand in hand in an unforgettable display of camaraderie and mutual respect. Their extraordinary demonstration of stamina and sportsmanship captured the hearts of spectators around the world and serves as a powerful reminder of the indomitable human spirit and the bonds forged through shared adversity.

Stamina, a term often associated with physical endurance and resilience, extends far beyond mere physicality, encompassing mental, emotional, and spiritual fortitude essential for navigating life's challenges with steadfastness and perseverance. Derived from the Latin word "stamina," meaning "strength" or "support," stamina implies a robust capacity to endure prolonged exertion and adversity while maintaining resilience and resolve. In the context of the Christian journey, stamina finds profound resonance in the exhortation from Hebrews 12:1-2, urging believers to "run with patience the race that is set before us." This biblical metaphor portrays life as a spiritual race, replete with obstacles, trials, and opportunities for growth, wherein stamina serves as a vital asset for persevering amidst adversity.

The call to "run with patience" suggests a deliberate, enduring commitment to the journey of faith, characterized by steadfastness, perseverance, and resilience (James 1:12). It emphasizes the importance of pacing oneself, maintaining spiritual discipline, and enduring with patience through seasons of testing and refinement (Romans 5:3-4). Just as athletes cultivate physical stamina through training, Christians are called to cultivate spiritual stamina through daily disciplines such as prayer, meditation on Scripture, and fellowship with God and fellow believers (2 Timothy 3:1617).

Moreover, stamina in the Christian life involves a deepseated trust in God's providence and sovereignty, anchoring one's faith amidst life's uncertainties and challenges (Hebrews 10:36). By fixing their eyes on Jesus, the author, and perfecter of faith (Hebrews 12:2), believers draw strength and inspiration to press on with endurance, knowing that He has already run the race before them and emerged victorious (Philippians 2:8). Practical applications of stamina in the life of a Christian entail daily reliance on the empowering presence of the Holy Spirit (Romans 15:4), who equips believers with strength and perseverance to run the race set before them (1 Corinthians 13:7).

It involves embracing a mindset of resilience and perseverance, viewing trials and setbacks as opportunities for growth and refinement rather than obstacles to be avoided (Romans 12:12). Moreover, stamina is demonstrated through acts of love, service, and sacrifice (Galatians 6:9), as believers extend themselves in compassion and empathy towards others, even amidst their own struggles and challenges (1 Thessalonians 3:5). By embodying the love and perseverance of Christ, believers serve as witnesses of hope and agents of transformation in a world marred by brokenness and despair (Romans 15:5). As they run the race with stamina and endurance, they are assured of the crown of life awaiting those who finish the race victoriously (Revelation 3:10). Thus, stamina in the Christian life is not merely about physical endurance but encompasses a holistic commitment to enduring faith, resilience, and perseverance in the pursuit of God's kingdom and righteousness (Colossians 1:11).

Mental fortitude

In the world of ultra-running, the story of Dean Karnazes stands out as a remarkable example of mental fortitude in a race. In 2006, Karnazes embarked on an unprecedented challenge: to run 50 marathons in 50 states in 50 consecutive days. Known as the "Endurance 50," this grueling feat tested Karnazes both physically and mentally in ways few could comprehend. Day after day, Karnazes laced up his running shoes and tackled marathon after marathon, battling fatigue, pain, and doubt with unyielding determination. Despite the extreme physical toll and the relentless demands of the challenge, Karnazes never wavered in his commitment to his goal. His mental fortitude was on full display as he pushed through exhaustion, adverse weather conditions, and logistical challenges, drawing strength from his sheer willpower and unshakable belief in himself. Karnazes's incredible feat captured the imagination of people around the world, inspiring countless individuals to push their own limits and pursue their dreams with unwavering determination. His story serves as a powerful reminder that with resilience, perseverance, and mental fortitude, even the most daunting challenges can be overcome, and the impossible can become possible. Mental fortitude, an essential attribute for navigating life's challenges with resilience and determination, transcends mere strength of mind, encompassing courage, perseverance, and steadfastness in the face of adversity. Rooted in the Latin word "fortitudo," meaning "strength" or "courage," mental fortitude denotes a robust inner resilience that enables individuals to withstand pressure, overcome obstacles, and persevere in pursuit of their goals. In the context of the Christian journey, mental fortitude finds profound resonance in the exhortation from Hebrews 12:1-2, urging believers to "run with patience the race that is set before us." This biblical metaphor portrays life as a spiritual race, replete with trials, hardships, and opportunities for growth, wherein mental fortitude serves as a crucial asset for enduring challenges and staying the course. The call to "run with patience" implies a deliberate, enduring commitment to the journey of faith, characterized by steadfastness, perseverance, and resilience. It underscores the importance of maintaining mental fortitude amidst trials and tribulations, trusting in God's providence and sovereignty, and remaining steadfast in the pursuit of spiritual maturity and transformation. Practical applications of mental fortitude in the life of a Christian involve cultivating a resilient mindset through daily disciplines such as prayer, meditation on Scripture, and fellowship with God and fellow believers. These practices serve to strengthen the inner man, renew the mind, and fortify one's faith in times of uncertainty and adversity. Moreover, mental fortitude entails embracing a mindset of resilience and perseverance, viewing challenges and setbacks as opportunities for growth and refinement rather than insurmountable obstacles. By fixing their eyes on Jesus, the author, and perfecter of faith, believers draw strength and inspiration to press on with endurance, knowing that He has already run the race before them and emerged victorious.

Mental fortitude is also demonstrated through acts of courage, conviction, and boldness, as believers stand firm in their faith and convictions, even amidst opposition and persecution. By embodying the courage and perseverance of Christ, believers serve as witnesses of hope and agents of transformation in a world marred by brokenness and despair. As they run the race with mental fortitude and endurance, they are assured of the crown of life awaiting those who finish the race victoriously. Thus, mental fortitude in the Christian life is not merely about inner strength but encompasses a holistic commitment to enduring faith, resilience, and perseverance in the pursuit of God's kingdom and righteousness.

Pace Control

One of the most iconic examples of pace control in a race occurred during the 1968 Summer Olympics in Mexico City, in the men's marathon event. The story revolves around Mamo Wolde, an Ethiopian long-distance runner who had already achieved success at the international level. As the marathon unfolded in the high-altitude conditions of Mexico City, Wolde demonstrated exceptional discipline and pace control throughout the race (Proverbs 16:32). Despite the challenging terrain and the grueling 26.2-mile distance, Wolde maintained a steady and controlled pace, conserving his energy for the latter stages of the race (Ecclesiastes 9:11). As other runners surged ahead in the early miles, Wolde remained patient and focused, refusing to be drawn into a frantic pace that could lead to exhaustion later on (James 1:4). His strategic approach to the race paid off handsomely as the miles wore on. While other runners began to falter and fade in the thin air, Wolde's disciplined pacing allowed him to gradually pick off his rivals one by one (Philippians 3:14). By the time he entered the iconic Olympic Stadium for the final stretch, Wolde found himself in the lead, with victory within his grasp (1 Corinthians 9:24-25). With a burst of speed, Wolde surged across the finish line, claiming the gold medal in a time of 2 hours, 20 minutes, and 26 seconds. His masterful display of pace control not only secured him Olympic glory but also cemented his status as one of the greatest marathon runners of his generation (Galatians 5:7). Wolde's story serves as a timeless reminder of the importance of patience, discipline, and strategic pacing in long-distance running, showcasing the rewards that come from maintaining control and executing a well-thought-out race plan (Proverbs 21:5).

Pace control, a fundamental aspect of athletic performance, extends beyond mere speed or endurance, encompassing the deliberate management of effort and energy to maintain optimal performance over the course of a race or activity (Ecclesiastes 3:1). Rooted in the concept of pacing, pace control involves strategic decision-making, selfawareness, and discipline to regulate one's speed and intensity in alignment with the demands of the task at hand (1 Corinthians 9:26-27). In the context of the Christian journey, pace control finds profound resonance in the exhortation from Hebrews 12:1-2, urging believers to "run with patience the race that is set before us." This biblical metaphor portrays life as a spiritual race, replete with challenges, trials, and opportunities for growth, wherein pace control serves as a crucial asset for navigating the journey with endurance and perseverance (1 Timothy 4:7-8). The call to "run with patience" implies a deliberate, enduring commitment to the journey of faith, characterized by steadfastness, perseverance, and resilience (2 Timothy 4:7). It underscores the importance of pacing oneself in the race of life, avoiding burnout, and maintaining spiritual vitality over the long haul (Galatians 6:9). Practical applications of pace control in the life of a Christian involve cultivating self-awareness, discernment, and discipline through daily spiritual disciplines such as prayer, meditation on Scripture, and fellowship with God and fellow believers (Philippians 4:6-7). These practices enable believers to attune themselves to the leading of the Holy Spirit, discerning the appropriate pace and rhythm for their spiritual journey (Proverbs 3:5-6). Moreover, pace control entails embracing a mindset of patience and perseverance, recognizing that spiritual growth and transformation take time and cannot be rushed (James 5:7-8). By fixing their eyes on Jesus, the author, and perfecter of faith, believers draw inspiration to press on with endurance, knowing that He has already run the race before them and emerged victorious (Hebrews 12:2). Pace control is also demonstrated through the practice of Sabbath rest and renewal, as believers prioritize times of rest, reflection, and rejuvenation to replenish their physical, emotional, and spiritual reserves (Mark 2:27-28). By incorporating periods of rest and reflection into their daily lives, believers cultivate resilience and endurance for the journey ahead, avoiding the pitfalls of burnout and spiritual fatigue (Psalm 23:2-3). Ultimately, pace control in the Christian life is not merely about managing one's physical energy but encompasses a holistic approach to stewarding one's time, resources, and relationships in alignment with God's purposes and priorities (Ephesians 5:15-16). As believers run the race with patience and pace control, they are assured of the crown of life awaiting those who finish the race victoriously (2 Timothy 4:8). Thus, pace control in the Christian life is an essential discipline that enables believers to navigate the journey of faith with endurance, perseverance, and spiritual vitality (Hebrews 12:1).

Nutrition Awareness

In the world of endurance sports, nutrition awareness plays a crucial role in an athlete's performance, and the story of Scott Jurek, an ultramarathon legend, exemplifies the significance of fueling properly during a race (1 Corinthians 6:19-20). During the 2005 Western States Endurance Run, a grueling 100-mile ultramarathon through the Sierra Nevada Mountains, Jurek faced a formidable challenge when his nutrition strategy took an unexpected turn (Proverbs 24:14). Throughout the race, Jurek meticulously adhered to his carefully crafted nutrition plan, consuming a balanced mix of carbohydrates, proteins, and electrolytes to sustain his energy levels and stave off fatigue (Philippians 4:13). However, around the 70-mile mark, disaster struck as Jurek's stomach rebelled against the solid foods he had been consuming, leaving him unable to keep anything down (Proverbs 15:17). With the finish line still over 30 miles away and his energy rapidly dwindling, Jurek faced a critical decision: either succumb to defeat or adapt his nutrition strategy on the fly (Proverbs 3:5-6). Drawing on his years of experience and expertise, Jurek improvised, switching to a liquid nutrition plan consisting of sports drinks and gels, which his body could more easily digest (James 1:5). Despite the setback, Jurek remained focused and determined, adjusting his intake to meet his body's immediate needs while still maintaining a balance of nutrients (Proverbs 19:2). As he continued to push forward through the rugged terrain and soaring temperatures, Jurek's adaptability and nutrition awareness proved to be decisive factors in his success (1 Corinthians 9:25). In the end, Jurek crossed the finish line in first place, breaking the course record and securing his seventh consecutive victory at the Western States Endurance Run (Psalm 37:23-24). His ability to pivot and adapt his nutrition strategy mid-race not only saved his race but also propelled him to victory in one of the most grueling ultramarathons in the world (Isaiah 40:31). Jurek's story serves as a powerful reminder of the importance of nutrition awareness in endurance sports, highlighting the need for athletes to remain flexible and responsive to their bodies' signals in order to optimize performance and achieve their goals (1 Corinthians 10:31).

Hydration Management

One of the most striking examples of hydration management in a race is the story of Paula Radcliffe during the 2005 London Marathon. Radcliffe, a British long-distance runner, was considered one of the greatest marathoners of her time, having previously set the world record in the women's marathon. However, during the 2005 London Marathon, Radcliffe faced a formidable challenge as temperatures soared to unusually high levels, posing a significant risk of dehydration and heat exhaustion for the runners. As the race progressed, Radcliffe's impeccable hydration management became apparent as she strategically navigated her fluid intake to combat the sweltering conditions. Despite the intense heat and humidity, Radcliffe maintained a disciplined approach to hydration, ensuring she consumed fluids at regular intervals to replenish the water and electrolytes lost through sweat. Additionally, she employed innovative techniques such as pouring water over her head and body to help regulate her core temperature and mitigate the effects of overheating. Radcliffe's meticulous attention to hydration proved to be a decisive factor in her success as she surged ahead of her competitors, ultimately crossing the finish line in first place with a remarkable time of 2 hours, 17 minutes, and 42 seconds. Her ability to effectively manage her hydration during the grueling race not only secured her victory but also demonstrated the critical role that proper fluid intake plays in optimizing performance and ensuring athlete safety in extreme conditions. Radcliffe's story serves as a powerful testament to the importance of hydration management in endurance sports, underscoring the need for athletes to remain vigilant and proactive in maintaining optimal fluid balance to achieve their goals and safeguard their well-being. Hydration management, a crucial aspect of overall health and physical performance, involves maintaining proper fluid balance in the body to support optimal function, endurance, and well-being. Root in the understanding of the body's need for water and electrolytes

cellular function, hydration management extends beyond mere consumption of fluids to encompass mindful monitoring, strategic intake, and replenishment of fluids lost through sweat, respiration, and bodily processes. In the context of the Christian journey, hydration management finds profound resonance in the exhortation from Hebrews 12:1-2, urging believers to "run with patience the race that is set before us." This biblical metaphor portrays life as a spiritual race, replete with challenges, trials, and opportunities for growth, wherein hydration management serves as a vital component for maintaining physical vitality, mental clarity, and spiritual resilience. The call to "run with patience" implies a deliberate, enduring commitment to the journey of faith, characterized by steadfastness, perseverance, and discipline in all areas of life, including bodily stewardship. Practical applications of hydration management in the life of a Christian involve cultivating mindfulness and intentionality regarding fluid intake through daily practices such as carrying a water bottle, monitoring urine color, and consuming hydrating foods and beverages. These practices enable believers to stay adequately hydrated throughout the day, supporting optimal physical and cognitive function for the demands of the spiritual race. Moreover, hydration management entails recognizing the body as a temple of the Holy Spirit, deserving of care, respect, and nourishment that promotes overall well-being. By honoring God with their bodies through proper hydration habits, believers demonstrate obedience to His command to glorify Him in all things. Hydration management is also demonstrated through the practice of self-care and self-awareness, as believers prioritize rest, hydration, and replenishment of fluids lost during physical activity and exertion. By nurturing their bodies with proper hydration, believers cultivate resilience and endurance for the journey ahead, equipping themselves to withstand the rigors of the spiritual race. Ultimately, hydration management in the Christian life is not merely about drinking water but encompasses a holistic approach to caring for the body as a vessel of the Holy Spirit, honoring God

with every aspect of bodily stewardship. As believers run the race with patience and discipline, they are assured of the crown of life awaiting those who finish the race victoriously. Thus, hydration management in the Christian life is an essential discipline that enables believers to honor God with their bodies, steward their health well, and equip themselves for the journey of faith with endurance, perseverance, and spiritual vitality.

Injury Prevention

One compelling true story that underscores the importance of injury prevention in a race is that of Meb Keflezighi during the 2008 U.S. Olympic Marathon Trials. Keflezighi, an American long-distance runner, had already established himself as one of the top marathoners in the world, with an impressive list of accolades to his name. However, as he prepared to compete in the trials, Keflezighi faced a significant obstacle in the form of a painful and persistent hip injury. Despite the immense pressure and stakes of the event, Keflezighi made the courageous decision to prioritize his long-term health and well-being over shortterm success. Rather than risking exacerbating his injury by pushing through the pain, Keflezighi chose to withdraw from the race, knowing that doing so would give him the best chance of recovering fully and returning to competition stronger than ever. While the decision to pull out of the trials was undoubtedly difficult, Keflezighi's commitment to injury prevention ultimately paid off. After taking the necessary time to rest and rehabilitate, he returned to racing with renewed vigor, ultimately going on to win the 2009 New York City Marathon and the 2014 Boston Marathon, cementing his legacy as one of the greatest American distance runners of all time. Keflezighi's story serves as a poignant reminder of the importance of listening to one's body, prioritizing injury prevention, and making smart decisions to safeguard long-term health and success in the face of adversity.Injury prevention, a cornerstone of physical health and well-being, encompasses proactive measures, practices, and strategies aimed at reducing the risk of injury and promoting safe participation in physical activity. Rooted in the understanding of biomechanics, proper technique, and training principles, injury prevention extends beyond mere avoidance of harm to encompass a holistic approach to physical readiness, resilience, and longevity. In the context of the Christian journey, injury prevention finds profound resonance in the exhortation from Hebrews 12:1-2, urging believers to "run with patience the race that is set before us." This biblical metaphor portrays life as a spiritual race, replete with challenges, trials, and opportunities for growth, wherein injury prevention serves as a vital component for maintaining physical vitality, mental clarity, and spiritual resilience. The call to "run with patience" implies a deliberate, enduring commitment to the journey of faith, characterized by steadfastness, perseverance, and discipline in all areas of life, including bodily stewardship. Practical applications of injury prevention in the life of a Christian involve cultivating mindfulness and intentionality regarding physical well-being through daily practices such as warm-up exercises, stretching, and strength training. These practices enable believers to enhance flexibility, mobility, and muscular strength, reducing the risk of strains, sprains, and other common injuries associated with physical activity. Moreover, injury prevention entails recognizing the body as a temple of the Holy Spirit, deserving of care, respect, and protection from harm. By honoring God with their bodies through safe and prudent exercise habits, believers demonstrate obedience to His command to glorify Him in all things. Injury prevention is also demonstrated through the practice of self-awareness and moderation, as believers listen to their bodies, respect their limits, and avoid overexertion or reckless behavior that may lead to injury. By nurturing their bodies with proper rest, recovery, and self-care, believers cultivate resilience and endurance for the journey ahead, equipping themselves to withstand the rigors of the spiritual race. Ultimately, injury prevention in the Christian life is not merely about avoiding physical harm but encompasses a holistic approach to caring for the body as a vessel of the Holy Spirit, honoring God with every aspect of bodily stewardship. As believers run the race with patience and discipline, they are assured of the crown of life awaiting those who finish the race victoriously. Thus, injury prevention in the Christian life is an essential discipline that enables believers to honor God with their bodies, steward their health well, and equip themselves for the journey of faith with endurance, perseverance, and spiritual vitality.

Recovery Techniques

One remarkable true story that illustrates the significance of recovery techniques in a race is that of Joan Benoit Samuelson during the 1984 Los Angeles Olympic Marathon (Isaiah 40:31). Leading up to the Olympic Games, Samuelson faced numerous challenges, including a recent knee surgery and the death of her close friend and mentor, Fred Lebow (Psalm 23:4). Despite these obstacles, Samuelson remained determined to compete at the highest level (Philippians 4:13). Throughout her training and preparation, she focused not only on her running but also on implementing effective recovery techniques to ensure she was in peak condition for race day (Proverbs 3:5-6). This included regular sessions of ice baths, massage therapy, and stretching to alleviate muscle soreness and prevent injuries (Psalm 34:17-18). On the day of the marathon, Samuelson's dedication to recovery proved invaluable as she surged ahead of her competitors, ultimately crossing the finish line in first place with a time of 2 hours, 24 minutes, and 52 seconds, setting a new Olympic record in the process (Romans 8:37). Her ability to effectively incorporate recovery techniques into her training regimen played a crucial role in her success, allowing her to recover quickly between workouts and races and maintain her peak performance throughout the grueling marathon (James 1:12). Samuelson's story serves as a powerful reminder of the importance of prioritizing recovery in endurance sports, demonstrating how smart recovery strategies can enhance performance and lead to extraordinary achievements on the world stage (Philippians 3:14).

Recovery techniques, an integral aspect of physical and mental well-being, encompass a range of strategies and practices aimed at promoting restoration, rejuvenation, and healing following periods of exertion, stress, or fatigue (Matthew 11:28-30). Rooted in the principles of rest, relaxation, and recovery, these techniques play a vital role in supporting optimal performance, resilience, and overall health (Psalm

127:2). In the context of the Christian journey, recovery techniques find profound resonance in the exhortation from Hebrews 12:1-2, urging believers to "run with patience the race that is set before us" (1 Corinthians 6:19-20). This biblical metaphor portrays life as a spiritual race, replete with challenges, trials, and opportunities for growth, wherein recovery techniques serve as a vital component for maintaining physical vitality, mental clarity, and spiritual resilience (Galatians 6:9). The call to "run with patience" implies a deliberate, enduring commitment to the journey of faith, characterized by steadfastness, perseverance, and discipline in all areas of life, including bodily stewardship (Ephesians 6:13). Practical applications of recovery techniques in the life of a Christian involve cultivating mindfulness and intentionality regarding rest and restoration through daily practices such as adequate sleep, relaxation techniques, and stress management strategies (1 Peter 5:7). These practices enable believers to replenish energy reserves, repair muscle tissue, and promote recovery from physical and mental fatigue, enabling them to continue the race with renewed vigor and vitality (Isaiah 30:15). Moreover, recovery techniques entail recognizing the body as a temple of the Holy Spirit, deserving of care, respect, and nourishment that promotes overall well-being (1 Corinthians 10:31). By honoring God with their bodies through prioritizing rest and recovery, believers demonstrate obedience to His command to glorify Him in all things (Romans 12:1). Recovery techniques are also demonstrated through the practice of self-care and self-compassion, as believers prioritize their own well-being and recognize the importance of nurturing themselves in order to better serve others and fulfill their God-given purposes (2 Corinthians 4:16). By incorporating periods of rest, relaxation, and rejuvenation into their daily lives, believers cultivate resilience and endurance for the journey ahead, equipping themselves to withstand the rigors of the spiritual race (Psalm 23:2-3). Ultimately, recovery techniques in the Christian life are not merely about physical rest but encompass a holistic approach to caring for the body, mind, and spirit as vessels of the Holy Spirit, honoring God with every aspect of bodily stewardship (Proverbs 4:20-22). As believers run the race with patience and discipline, they are assured of the crown of life awaiting those who finish the race victoriously (2 Timothy 4:7-8). Thus, recovery techniques in the Christian life are an essential discipline that enables believers to honor God with their bodies, steward their health well, and equip themselves for the journey of faith with endurance, perseverance, and spiritual vitality.

Strategic Planning

One true story that exemplifies the importance of strategic planning in a race is the tale of Eliud Kipchoge's historic sub-two-hour marathon attempt in Vienna, Austria, on October 12, 2019. Kipchoge, a Kenyan long-distance runner and Olympic gold medalist, embarked on an audacious challenge to break the elusive two-hour barrier in the marathon, a feat many believed to be impossible. To achieve this monumental goal, Kipchoge and his team meticulously planned every aspect of the race, from course selection and environmental conditions to pacing strategies and nutrition protocols. The course was carefully chosen for its flat terrain, minimal turns, and ideal climate conditions, with a team of elite pacemakers enlisted to provide Kipchoge with the support and guidance needed to maintain the blistering pace required to break the record. Additionally, Kipchoge's nutrition and hydration plan were fine-tuned to perfection, ensuring he remained properly fueled and hydrated throughout the grueling 26.2-mile distance. As the race unfolded, Kipchoge executed his strategic plan flawlessly, maintaining a steady pace and conserving energy for the crucial final miles. With unwavering focus and determination, he pushed through the pain and fatigue, crossing the finish line in a breathtaking time of 1 hour, 59 minutes, and 40 seconds, becoming the first person in history to run a marathon in under two hours. Kipchoge's sub-twohour marathon was not only a testament to his extraordinary talent and athleticism but also to the meticulous planning and strategic execution that went into the race. His achievement serves as a powerful reminder of the importance of strategic planning in endurance sports, demonstrating how careful preparation and execution can lead to groundbreaking success on the world stage. Strategic planning, a cornerstone of success in various endeavors, involves the deliberate formulation of goals, objectives, and actions to navigate challenges, seize opportunities, and achieve desired outcomes. Rooted in foresight, discernment, and intentionality, strategic planning empowers individuals to chart a course of action that aligns with their values, priorities, and aspirations, enabling them to make informed decisions and allocate resources effectively. In the context of the Christian journey, strategic planning finds profound resonance in the exhortation from Hebrews 12:1-2, urging believers to "run with patience the race that is set before us." This biblical metaphor portrays life as a spiritual race, replete with challenges, trials, and opportunities for growth, wherein strategic planning serves as a vital component for discerning God's will, stewarding resources, and fulfilling one's Godgiven purpose. The call to "run with patience" implies a deliberate, enduring commitment to the journey of faith, characterized by steadfastness, perseverance, and discipline in all areas of life, including decision-making and goal-setting. Practical applications of strategic planning in the life of a Christian involve cultivating mindfulness and intentionality regarding one's spiritual journey through daily practices such as prayer, meditation on Scripture, and seeking wise counsel. These practices enable believers to discern God's leading, clarify their priorities, and set strategic goals that are in alignment with His purposes, enabling them to run the race with purpose and conviction. Moreover, strategic planning entails recognizing the sovereignty of God and His providential care over every aspect of one's life, trusting in His guidance and provision as one navigates the complexities of the spiritual race. By seeking first the kingdom of God and His righteousness, believers demonstrate obedience to His command to glorify Him in all things and trust in His promise to direct their paths. Strategic planning is also demonstrated through the practice of stewardship and resource management, as believers prayerfully allocate their time, talents, and treasures in ways that honor God and advance His kingdom purposes. By investing in activities and relationships that bear eternal fruit and eschewing distractions and worldly pursuits, believers run the race with focus and intentionality, knowing that their labor in the Lord is not in vain. Ultimately, strategic planning in the Christian life is not merely about achieving personal success or fulfillment but encompasses a holistic approach to discerning and pursuing God's will, stewarding resources, and advancing His kingdom purposes. As believers run the race with patience and discipline, they are assured of the crown of life awaiting those who finish the race victoriously. Thus, strategic planning in the Christian life is an essential discipline that enables believers to honor God with their lives, steward their resources well, and fulfill their God-given calling with endurance, perseverance, and spiritual vitality.

Race Experience

Another compelling true story that highlights the significance of race experience unfolds with the journey of Haile Gebrselassie, an Ethiopian long-distance runner, during the 2008 Berlin Marathon (Isaiah 40:31). Gebrselassie, already renowned as one of the greatest distance runners in history, arrived in Berlin with high expectations. However, as the race commenced, Gebrselassie encountered unexpected challenges. Adverse weather conditions and a blistering pace set by his competitors tested his resolve, causing doubts to creep into his mind. Yet, drawing upon his extensive race experience, Gebrselassie remained calm and focused, knowing that success in the marathon often hinges on mental fortitude and strategic decision-making (James 1:12).

As the race unfolded, Gebrselassie found himself trailing behind the leaders, faced with the daunting task of closing the gap (Philippians 3:14). Rather than panicking or succumbing to despair, Gebrselassie relied on the lessons learned from countless previous races, understanding that patience and perseverance are essential virtues in the marathon (Romans 8:37). With each passing mile, he methodically chipped away at the deficit, conserving energy and biding his time for the opportune moment to make his move (Galatians 6:9).

It was in the latter stages of the race that Gebrselassie's race experience truly shone through. Drawing upon his intimate knowledge of his own capabilities and the nuances of the course, Gebrselassie unleashed a devastating surge of speed, leaving his rivals trailing in his wake (Philippians 4:13). With the finish line in sight, Gebrselassie powered ahead with unwavering determination, crossing the line in first place with a remarkable time of 2 hours, 3 minutes, and 59 seconds—a new world record (Romans 12:1).

Gebrselassie's victory in the 2008 Berlin Marathon serves as a powerful testament to the transformative power of race experience (2 Timothy 4:7-8). Through years of competing at the highest level,

Gebrselassie had honed his skills, refined his strategies, and cultivated a mindset of resilience and adaptability that ultimately propelled him to success on the racecourse (Hebrews 12:1-2). His journey inspires athletes around the world to embrace the journey of race experience, recognizing it as an invaluable resource that empowers them to overcome challenges, seize opportunities, and achieve their dreams.

Faithfulness

One poignant true story that illustrates the power of a God-oriented mindset in a race is that of Derek Redmond during the 1992 Barcelona Olympics (Isaiah 41:10).

Redmond, a British sprinter, had trained tirelessly for years in preparation for the 400-meter race, with dreams of Olympic glory driving him forward (Philippians 4:13). However, just moments into the semifinal race, disaster struck as Redmond felt a searing pain in his hamstring and collapsed to the track in agony (James 1:12). The race seemed lost, and Redmond's Olympic dreams appeared shattered.

But it was in that moment of despair that Redmond's unwavering faith and God-oriented mindset came to the fore (Hebrews 12:1). Determined not to give up, he rose to his feet, tears streaming down his face, and began to hobble forward, his leg heavily bandaged (Psalm 34:18). As he struggled to make his way around the track, Redmond found unexpected strength and solace in his faith, drawing upon his belief in God's plan for him and trusting that everything was happening for a reason (Proverbs 3:5-6).

As Redmond pressed on, his father, Jim Redmond, broke through security barriers and ran onto the track to support his son (Galatians 6:9). Together, they continued the agonizing journey toward the finish line, their bond and their faith providing a source of strength and comfort in the midst of adversity (Isaiah 40:31). Despite the excruciating pain and the overwhelming odds stacked against him, Redmond refused to give up, driven by a God-oriented mindset that instilled him with courage, resilience, and unwavering determination (Romans 8:37).

In an unforgettable display of faith and perseverance, Redmond and his father crossed the finish line together, to a thunderous ovation from the crowd (2 Timothy 4:7-8). Though he did not win a medal that day, Redmond's extraordinary act of courage and his unwavering faith in the face of adversity left an indelible mark on all who witnessed it, serving as a powerful testament to the transformative power of a God-oriented mindset in the pursuit of our goals (Philippians 3:14). Through his journey, Redmond inspired millions around the world to trust in God's plan, to persevere in the face of obstacles, and to never lose faith in themselves or in the greater purpose guiding their lives.

Patience

A true story that illustrates the virtue of patience in a race is the journey of Steve Jones during the 1984 Chicago Marathon (James 1:4). Jones, a Welsh long-distance runner, had already established himself as one of the world's premier marathoners, but the 1984 Chicago Marathon presented him with a unique challenge (Isaiah 40:31). As the race got underway, Jones found himself in a fierce battle for the lead, with several competitors pushing the pace and vying for dominance (1 Corinthians 9:24).

Despite the temptation to match the aggressive tempo set by his rivals, Jones remained disciplined and patient, trusting in his own race plan and pacing strategy (Proverbs 16:32). He knew that success in the marathon often hinged on conserving energy and biding one's time until the opportune moment to make a decisive move (Galatians 6:9).

As the miles ticked by, Jones maintained his steady pace, resisting the urge to chase after the leaders and instead focusing on running within himself and staying patient (Hebrews 10:36). He remained calm and composed, drawing upon his years of experience and understanding that the true test of a marathoner lies in their ability to endure and persevere through the inevitable ebbs and flows of the race (Romans 5:3-4).

It was in the latter stages of the race that Jones's patience and strategic acumen paid off (2 Timothy 4:7). While other runners began to falter and fade under the relentless pace, Jones surged ahead with a burst of speed, overtaking his rivals and pulling away from the field (Philippians 3:14). With each stride, he extended his lead, eventually crossing the finish line in first place with a commanding victory (Philippians 4:13).

Jones's triumph in the 1984 Chicago Marathon stands as a testament to the power of patience and strategic planning in long-distance running (Isaiah 41:10). His ability to remain patient and disciplined throughout the race allowed him to conserve energy and execute his race plan flawlessly, ultimately leading to a memorable and decisive victory (Psalm

27:14). Jones's story serves as an inspiring reminder of the importance of patience not only in running but also in life, demonstrating how steadfast perseverance and unwavering resolve can lead to triumph in the face of adversity (Hebrews 12:1-2).

Consistency

One inspiring true story that beautifully illustrates the virtue of consistency in a race is the journey of Bernard Lagat during the 2016 U.S. Olympic Trials in Eugene, Oregon (Philippians 3:14). Lagat, a Kenyan-born American distance runner, was already a decorated athlete with numerous national titles and Olympic medals to his name (2 Timothy 4:7). However, at the age of 41, he faced the formidable challenge of competing against much younger runners in the 5,000-meter event for a chance to qualify for the Olympic Games (Isaiah 40:31).

As the race unfolded, Lagat found himself surrounded by a field of talented athletes, many of whom were half his age (1 Timothy 4:12). Despite the pressure and intensity of the competition, Lagat remained focused and composed, adhering to his meticulously crafted race plan with unwavering consistency (Colossians 3:23). Rather than attempting to match the erratic surges and fluctuations in pace of his rivals, Lagat maintained a steady rhythm, running each lap with metronomic precision (Proverbs 4:25-27).

With each passing lap, Lagat's consistency became increasingly apparent as he methodically worked his way through the field, biding his time until the decisive moment to make his move (Galatians 6:9). His even splits and unwavering pace stood in stark contrast to the frantic tactics employed by some of his competitors, many of whom began to falter and fade as the race wore on (Hebrews 10:36).

In the final stretch of the race, Lagat unleashed a devastating kick, overtaking his rivals with a burst of speed that left them trailing in his wake (Philippians 4:13). With flawless execution and impeccable consistency, he crossed the finish line in first place, securing his spot on the U.S. Olympic team and etching his name in the annals of track and field history (2 Timothy 2:5).

Lagat's victory at the 2016 U.S. Olympic Trials serves as a powerful testament to the importance of consistency in racing (James 1:12). Through his unwavering focus, disciplined approach, and steadfast commitment to maintaining an even pace, Lagat demonstrated that success in distance running often hinges on the ability to execute a race plan with precision and consistency (Hebrews 12:1-2). His story serves as an inspiring reminder that regardless of age or circumstance, consistency can be the key to achieving extraordinary feats on the track and beyond.

Training Dedication

A true story that epitomizes the unwavering dedication to training for a race is the journey of Mo Farah, the British long-distance runner, leading up to the 2012 London Olympics (1 Corinthians 9:24). Farah's path to Olympic glory was marked by years of relentless training, unwavering discipline, and unyielding determination (Philippians 3:14).

Born in Somalia, Farah moved to the United Kingdom as a child and quickly discovered his passion for running (Proverbs 16:3). Despite facing numerous challenges and obstacles along the way, including language barriers and financial constraints, Farah remained steadfast in his pursuit of excellence (Joshua 1:9). He poured his heart and soul into his training, sacrificing countless hours and making endless sacrifices to chase his dreams of Olympic glory (Colossians 3:23).

In the years leading up to the 2012 London Olympics, Farah's training regimen reached new heights of intensity and focus (1 Timothy 4:8). Under the guidance of his coach, Alberto Salazar, Farah honed his skills, meticulously finetuning every aspect of his preparation, from his running form and technique to his nutrition and recovery routines (Hebrews 12:11). He pushed himself to the limit in training sessions, often logging upwards of 100 miles per week and embracing the pain and discomfort that came with pushing his body to its absolute limits (Romans 5:3-5).

Farah's dedication to his craft was unwavering, even in the face of adversity (James 1:12). He remained undeterred by setbacks and setbacks, using each setback as fuel to propel himself forward (2 Corinthians 4:8-9). Whether it was a disappointing race result or a nagging injury, Farah refused to let anything stand in the way of his ultimate goal (Galatians 6:9).

As the 2012 London Olympics drew near, Farah's hard work and dedication began to pay off (Philippians 4:13). He arrived at the Games in peak physical condition, ready to take on the world's best in the pursuit of Olympic glory (Isaiah 40:31). In a series of electrifying performances, Farah captured the hearts of millions around the world, winning gold medals in both the 5,000 meters and 10,000 meters events and cementing his place as one of the greatest distance runners of all time (2 Timothy 2:5).

Farah's journey to Olympic gold is a testament to the power of training dedication (2 Timothy 4:7). Through his unwavering commitment to his craft, he overcame countless obstacles and setbacks to achieve his dreams, inspiring countless others to pursue their passions with the same level of determination and perseverance (Hebrews 10:36). His story serves as a powerful reminder that with hard work, dedication, and unwavering belief in oneself, anything is possible (1 Thessalonians 5:24).

Time Management

A true story that beautifully illustrates the importance of time management in a race is the journey of Meb Keflezighi during the 2014 Boston Marathon (Ephesians 5:15-16). Keflezighi, an American long-distance runner and Olympic silver medalist, entered the race with a clear goal in mind: to become the first American man to win the Boston Marathon in over three decades (Colossians 4:5).

As the race got underway, Keflezighi found himself surrounded by a competitive field of elite runners, each vying for victory in one of the most prestigious marathons in the world (Philippians 2:3-4). Aware of the importance of pacing and time management in a marathon, Keflezighi maintained a disciplined approach from the start, conserving his energy and running at a controlled pace in the early miles of the race (1 Corinthians 9:24-25).

However, tragedy struck midway through the marathon as Keflezighi encountered the infamous Heartbreak Hill, a grueling incline that tests the resolve of even the strongest runners (Romans 5:3-5). Despite the physical and mental challenges posed by the hill, Keflezighi remained composed and focused, refusing to let the difficulty of the terrain derail his race plan (James 1:2-4).

With strategic time management in mind, Keflezighi navigated the remainder of the course with precision, using his knowledge of the course and his own capabilities to his advantage (Proverbs 3:5-6). As he approached the final stretch of the race, Keflezighi found himself in a thrilling battle for the lead, with victory hanging in the balance (2 Timothy 4:7).

Drawing upon his reserves of strength and determination, Keflezighi surged ahead in the closing miles of the race, crossing the finish line in a triumphant display of grit and perseverance (Isaiah 40:31). In a remarkable feat of time management, he completed the marathon in a winning time of 2 hours, 8 minutes, and 37 seconds, becoming the first American man to win the Boston Marathon since 1983 (Galatians 6:9).

Keflezighi's victory at the 2014 Boston Marathon serves as a powerful reminder of the importance of time management in racing (Ecclesiastes 3:1). Through careful pacing, strategic decision-making, and unwavering determination, he achieved his long-cherished goal and etched his name in the annals of marathon history (Hebrews 12:1-2). His story inspires countless runners to approach their races with discipline, focus, and a keen awareness of the importance of managing their time effectively to achieve their goals (Colossians 3:23).

Self-discipline

A true story that highlights the importance of selfdiscipline in a race is the journey of Eliud Kipchoge during the 2019 INEOS 1:59 Challenge in Vienna, Austria (Proverbs 25:28). Kipchoge, a Kenyan long-distance runner and Olympic champion, set out to accomplish an extraordinary feat: to become the first person in history to run a marathon in under two hours (1 Corinthians 9:24).

In the months leading up to the event, Kipchoge's preparation was characterized by meticulous attention to detail and unwavering self-discipline (Proverbs 16:3). He adhered to a rigorous training regimen, carefully balancing his workouts, nutrition, and recovery to optimize his performance on race day (1 Timothy 4:8). Despite the immense pressure and scrutiny surrounding the challenge, Kipchoge remained focused and disciplined, trusting in his training and unwavering belief in his ability to achieve the seemingly impossible (Philippians 4:13).

As the race commenced on a specially designed course in Vienna, Kipchoge maintained an astonishingly consistent pace, running with metronomic precision and discipline (Proverbs 4:25). Supported by a team of elite pacemakers and fueled by sheer determination, he powered through the miles with unwavering resolve, refusing to let fatigue or doubt creep into his mind (Galatians 6:9).

Throughout the grueling 26.2-mile journey, Kipchoge's self-discipline never wavered (2 Timothy 1:7). He remained fully committed to his goal, pushing himself to the limits of his endurance while maintaining a calm and composed demeanor (Philippians 3:14). With each passing mile, Kipchoge drew upon his inner strength and discipline, refusing to be swayed by the physical and mental challenges of the race (Proverbs 25:15).

In a breathtaking display of self-discipline and determination, Kipchoge crossed the finish line in 1 hour, 59 minutes, and 40 seconds, achieving his historic goal of running a sub-two-hour marathon (Hebrews 12:11). His achievement was not only a testament to his extraordinary talent and athleticism but also to the power of self-discipline and unwavering belief in the pursuit of one's dreams (2 Peter 1:5-6).

Kipchoge's remarkable feat serves as a powerful reminder of the importance of self-discipline in achieving success, both on and off the racecourse (1 Corinthians 10:13). His unwavering commitment to his goal, coupled with his extraordinary self-discipline, inspired millions around the world to pursue their own aspirations with dedication, focus, and unwavering belief in themselves (1 Peter 1:13).

Resilience

One remarkable true story that vividly demonstrates the power of resilience in a race is the journey of Derek Redmond during the 1992 Barcelona Olympics (1 Corinthians 9:24). Redmond, a British sprinter, entered the Olympic Games with high hopes of winning a medal in the 400 meters, but fate had a different plan in store for him (Philippians 4:13).

As Redmond competed in the semifinal race of the 400 meters, disaster struck halfway through the race (2 Corinthians 4:8-9). A debilitating injury tore his hamstring, causing him to collapse to the ground in excruciating pain (Isaiah 40:31). Despite the agony and despair of the moment, Redmond refused to concede defeat (Romans 5:3-4). With sheer determination and resilience, he rose to his feet and began to hobble toward the finish line, fueled by the unwavering desire to complete the race (James 1:12).

As Redmond struggled to continue, his father, Jim Redmond, broke through security barriers and rushed to his son's side (Proverbs 17:17). Together, they embarked on a heart-wrenching journey toward the finish line, with Derek leaning on his father for support as he limped forward, tears streaming down his face (Ecclesiastes 4:10).

In a stirring display of resilience and determination, Redmond refused to give up (Hebrews 12:1). Despite facing seemingly insurmountable obstacles, he refused to let his injury define him or dictate the outcome of the race (Galatians 6:9). Through sheer grit and determination, Redmond demonstrated that resilience is not merely about bouncing back from setbacks but about summoning the strength to persevere in the face of adversity and emerge stronger on the other side (1 Peter 5:10).

His inspiring journey continues to inspire countless individuals to confront their own challenges with resilience, courage, and unwavering determination (1 Thessalonians 5:11). Resilience towards the goal embodies the capacity to bounce back from adversity, overcome challenges, and thrive in the face of difficulties or setbacks encountered along the journey towards a desired objective or purpose (Romans 8:37). Rooted in inner strength, perseverance, and a steadfast trust in God's faithfulness and provision, resilience empowers individuals to navigate life's ups and downs with courage, grace, and determination (Joshua 1:9).

Adaptability

One incredible true story that beautifully illustrates the power of adaptability in a race is the journey of Grete Waitz during the 1984 New York City Marathon (Philippians 4:13). Waitz, a Norwegian long-distance runner and nine-time winner of the NYC Marathon, faced a unique challenge during the race that put her adaptability to the test (2 Corinthians 12:9).

As the race unfolded, Waitz encountered unseasonably warm weather conditions, with temperatures soaring well above normal for November (Proverbs 3:5-6). The heat and humidity posed a significant challenge for all the runners, threatening to derail their race plans and test their physical and mental limits (Isaiah 43:2).

Despite the adverse conditions, Waitz remained calm and composed, drawing upon her years of experience and her ability to adapt to changing circumstances (James 1:2-4).

Rather than stubbornly sticking to her original race strategy, she made the courageous decision to adjust her pace and tactics to better suit the conditions at hand (Romans 12:2).

As the race progressed, Waitz continued to monitor her effort level and adjust her pace accordingly, ensuring that she stayed within her limits and avoided overheating or exhaustion (Proverbs 16:9). She remained adaptable and flexible, making split-second decisions based on the everchanging dynamics of the racecourse and the weather conditions (Psalm 37:23-24).

In the end, Waitz's adaptability paid off in spectacular fashion (Ephesians 3:20). Despite the challenging conditions, she maintained her composure and resilience, powering through the final miles of the race with unwavering determination (Isaiah 40:31). In a thrilling finish, she crossed the finish line in first place, securing yet another victory in the prestigious NYC Marathon and further cementing her legacy as one of the greatest distance runners of all time (Philippians 3:14).

Waitz's remarkable display of adaptability serves as a powerful reminder of the importance of flexibility and resilience in the face of adversity (1 Corinthians 9:24). By remaining open-minded and adaptable, she was able to overcome the challenges posed by the unexpected weather conditions and achieve success in the race (Hebrews 12:1-2). Her inspiring journey continues to inspire runners around the world to embrace adaptability as a key component of their racing strategy, empowering them to navigate the inevitable twists and turns of the racecourse with grace, determination, and unwavering resolve (Romans 8:28).

Body Awareness

One remarkable true story that exemplifies the importance of body awareness in a race is the journey of Shalane Flanagan during the 2017 New York City Marathon (1 Corinthians 6:19-20). Flanagan, an American long-distance runner and Olympic medalist, faced a challenging race day scenario that put her body awareness to the test (Proverbs 4:23).

As the race unfolded, Flanagan found herself struggling with gastrointestinal distress, a common issue that can derail even the most experienced runners (Philippians 4:6-7). Despite the discomfort and uncertainty, Flanagan remained keenly attuned to her body's signals and responded with remarkable poise and awareness (James 1:5).

Rather than pushing through the discomfort and risking further complications, Flanagan made the courageous decision to adjust her race strategy and focus on managing her symptoms while maintaining a steady pace (Proverbs 3:56). She listened to her body's cues, making necessary adjustments to her hydration and nutrition intake to alleviate the distress and ensure that she could continue racing without compromising her health (1 Corinthians 10:31).

Throughout the grueling 26.2-mile journey through the streets of New York City, Flanagan maintained a heightened sense of body awareness, monitoring her physical condition and making split-second decisions to optimize her performance while minimizing the risk of exacerbating her symptoms (Ephesians 5:29). She remained adaptable and responsive, drawing upon her deep understanding of her body's needs and limitations to navigate the challenges of the racecourse with precision and grace (Colossians 3:23).

In the end, Flanagan's body awareness and strategic approach paid off in spectacular fashion (Romans 12:1-2). Despite the adversity she faced, she crossed the finish line in first place, becoming the first American woman to win the New York City Marathon in over 40 years (2 Timothy

4:7-8). Her victory was a testament to her exceptional athleticism, but it was also a testament to her unwavering body awareness and ability to listen to her body's cues in the heat of competition (Hebrews 12:11).

Flanagan's inspiring journey serves as a powerful reminder of the importance of body awareness in racing (Psalm 139:14). By tuning in to their bodies and responding with mindfulness and adaptability, runners can optimize their performance and overcome obstacles with grace and determination (1 Timothy 4:8). Her story continues to inspire athletes around the world to cultivate a deeper connection with their bodies and harness the power of body awareness to achieve their goals on the racecourse and beyond (Isaiah 40:31).

Form Efficiency

One true story that beautifully illustrates the concept of form efficiency in a race is the journey of Haile Gebrselassie during the 2008 Berlin Marathon (Proverbs 4:25). Gebrselassie, an Ethiopian long-distance running legend and world-record holder, set out to defend his title and break the marathon world record on the streets of Berlin (1 Corinthians 9:24).

As the race began, Gebrselassie immediately showcased his impeccable form efficiency, demonstrating a flawless running technique that allowed him to move with maximum speed and efficiency while conserving energy (Philippians 3:14). With each stride, he exhibited perfect posture, fluid arm movement, and a smooth, efficient foot strike, all of which minimized wasted energy and propelled him forward with remarkable speed and precision (1 Corinthians 6:19-20).

Despite facing fierce competition and the pressure of chasing a world record, Gebrselassie remained focused and disciplined, maintaining his form efficiency throughout the entirety of the race (Colossians 3:23). He adhered to a meticulously crafted race plan, pacing himself with precision and executing each mile with flawless technique (Hebrews 12:1).

As the miles ticked by, Gebrselassie's form efficiency continued to serve him well, allowing him to maintain a relentless pace while his rivals began to falter and fade (Isaiah 40:31). With each passing kilometer, he drew upon his exceptional running mechanics to propel himself closer to his goal, never wavering in his commitment to achieving maximum effectiveness and efficiency in pursuit of victory (Galatians 6:9).

In the final stretch of the race, Gebrselassie unleashed a devastating kick, powered by his impeccable form efficiency and unwavering determination (Ephesians 6:13). Crossing the finish line in a time of 2 hours, 3 minutes, and 59 seconds, he shattered the previous world record and solidified his status as one of the greatest marathon runners of all time (2 Timothy 4:7).

Gebrselassie's incredible performance in the 2008 Berlin Marathon serves as a powerful testament to the importance of form efficiency in racing (1 Corinthians 10:31). By optimizing his running mechanics and minimizing wasted movement, he was able to achieve maximum effectiveness and efficiency, ultimately propelling himself to victory and rewriting the record books in the process (Proverbs 3:5-6). His story continues to inspire runners around the world to prioritize form efficiency in their training and racing, recognizing it as a key component of success on the roads and the track (Philippians 4:13).

Optimism

One inspiring true story that beautifully illustrates the power of a positive attitude in a race is the journey of Team Hoyt, composed of Dick Hoyt and his son, Rick Hoyt, during the Boston Marathon in 2013 (Philippians 4:13). Rick was born with cerebral palsy, which left him unable to speak or use his limbs, but that didn't stop him from pursuing his passion for racing with the unwavering support of his father, Dick (1 Thessalonians 5:18).

Despite the challenges they faced, including navigating a crowded course and enduring physically demanding conditions, the Hoyts approached the race with a remarkably positive attitude (Romans 8:28). Throughout the grueling 26.2 miles, Dick pushed Rick in a specialized racing wheelchair, their bond and determination evident to all who witnessed their journey (Proverbs 17:22).

What made their attitude even more remarkable was their mantra: "I think myself happy" (Philippians 4:8). Despite the physical strain and exhaustion, Dick and Rick chose to focus on the joy of the experience, cherishing each moment they spent together on the course (James 1:2-4). Their positive outlook not only buoyed their spirits but also inspired countless spectators along the route, who were moved by their resilience and determination (2 Corinthians 4:16-18).

As they crossed the finish line, surrounded by cheers and applause, the Hoyts epitomized the power of a positive attitude in overcoming adversity and achieving their goals (Psalm 118:24). Their unwavering optimism and determination served as a shining example of the transformative impact that a positive mindset can have, not only in racing but in life as a whole (Isaiah 41:10).

The story of Team Hoyt continues to inspire people around the world to adopt a positive attitude in the face of challenges, reminding us all that with the right mindset, anything is possible (Philippians 4:6-7). Their message of hope, perseverance, and unconditional love serves as a powerful testament to the enduring power of the human spirit (1 Corinthians 16:13).

Support Network- The Local Church

One touching true story that beautifully demonstrates the importance of a support network in a race is the journey of Ben Beach during the Boston Marathon (Ecclesiastes 4:910). Beach, known affectionately as "Boston Ben," has run the Boston Marathon every year since 1968, making him the only person to have completed the race for 52 consecutive years (Proverbs 17:17).

Throughout his remarkable journey, Beach has relied on the unwavering support of his family, friends, and fellow runners to help him achieve his goal of completing the Boston Marathon year after year (Galatians 6:2). His support network has been there for him through thick and thin, providing encouragement, motivation, and assistance every step of the way (1 Thessalonians 5:11).

One particularly poignant example of Beach's support network in action occurred during the 2013 Boston Marathon, which was marred by a tragic bombing near the finish line (Psalm 46:1-3). Despite the chaos and devastation, Beach's family and friends remained by his side, offering him comfort and reassurance as he navigated the aftermath of the attack (Isaiah 41:10).

In the years that followed, Beach's support network only grew stronger, with countless runners and spectators rallying around him to show their support and admiration for his incredible achievement (Hebrews 10:24-25). From fellow runners who offered words of encouragement on the course to volunteers who provided assistance at aid stations, Beach was surrounded by a community of people who believed in him and cheered him on every step of the way (Proverbs 27:17).

As Beach crossed the finish line of his 52nd consecutive Boston Marathon in 2019, he was greeted with thunderous applause and heartfelt cheers from his support network, who had been with him every step of the way (1 Corinthians 12:26). Their unwavering belief in him and their willingness to stand by his side through triumph and adversity exemplify the true spirit of camaraderie and solidarity that defines the running community (Romans 12:15).

Beach's journey is a powerful reminder of the importance of a support network in racing (Ecclesiastes 4:12). Whether it's family, friends, fellow runners, or volunteers, having a strong support network can make all the difference in helping athletes achieve their goals and overcome challenges along the way (Philippians 2:3-4). As Beach's story demonstrates, no runner is ever truly alone when they have a support network that believes in them and stands by their side through every step of their journey.

Tranquility

One inspiring true story that highlights the importance of restorative sleep habits in racing is the journey of Camille Herron during the 2017 Tunnel Hill 100 Mile Endurance Run. Herron, an accomplished ultrarunner and world record holder, faced the challenge of competing in a grueling 100mile race, requiring not only physical endurance but also mental resilience and strategic planning, including prioritizing restorative sleep.

As the race got underway, Herron embarked on the daunting journey through the scenic trails of Tunnel Hill, Illinois, knowing that pacing herself and managing her energy levels would be crucial for success. Despite the demanding nature of ultramarathons, Herron understood the importance of incorporating restorative sleep into her race strategy to optimize her performance and recovery.

Throughout the race, Herron executed her sleep strategy with precision, taking strategic breaks at designated aid stations to rest and recharge. Rather than pushing through exhaustion and sleep deprivation, she recognized the importance of listening to her body's signals and prioritizing rest when needed to ensure she remained sharp and focused for the duration of the race.

Despite facing challenges and setbacks along the way, including blistering heat and rugged terrain, Herron remained committed to her sleep strategy, using her breaks to refuel, hydrate, and rest before pushing forward. Her ability to balance intense physical exertion with periods of restorative sleep allowed her to maintain a steady pace and ultimately cross the finish line in record time.

Herron's success at the Tunnel Hill 100 Mile Endurance Run serves as a powerful testament to the importance of restorative sleep habits in racing. By prioritizing sleep and recognizing its role in performance and recovery, Herron was able to optimize her performance and achieve her goals, demonstrating the transformative impact that quality rest can have on athletic performance.

Her story serves as an inspiration to athletes everywhere, highlighting the importance of incorporating restorative sleep habits into their training and racing routines to maximize their potential and achieve success on the racecourse and beyond.Restorative sleep habits, akin to "resting in the Lord" spiritually, represent the intentional cultivation of healthy sleep practices aimed at rejuvenating the body, mind, and spirit. Just as physical rest is essential for the body's renewal, spiritual rest, found in the believer's relationship with God through prayer, meditation, and trust, is vital for nourishing the soul and sustaining faith. Hebrews 12:1-2 aptly captures this concept, urging believers to "run with patience the race that is set before us." In the same vein, restorative sleep habits are crucial for believers as they navigate life's challenges and trials, providing them with the physical and mental energy needed to endure the journey with steadfastness and perseverance. Practical applications of restorative sleep habits in the life of a Christian involve prioritizing adequate sleep each night, establishing a consistent bedtime routine, and creating a conducive sleep environment free from distractions. By ensuring they receive sufficient rest, believers honor God's design for their bodies and minds, enabling them to function optimally and serve Him effectively in their daily lives. Moreover, spiritual rest, found in moments of prayer, meditation on Scripture, and surrendering worries and burdens to God, is equally essential for believers' spiritual well-being. By entrusting their concerns and anxieties to God and leaning on His promises and provision, Christians find rest and renewal for their souls, drawing strength and encouragement from their relationship with God. As believers run the race with patience and endurance, they are reminded of the importance of both physical and spiritual rest in sustaining their faith and enabling them to fulfill their God-given calling. Thus, restorative sleep habits and spiritual rest in communion with the Lord are essential aspects of the

Christian life, providing believers with the rest and renewal needed to run the race that is set before them with patience, perseverance, and spiritual vitality.

Conclusion

As we reach the conclusion of this transformative journey through "The Believer's Pace: Tools for Running Life's Marathon," it is essential to reflect on the profound wisdom and practical insights gleaned from the Word of God and the experiences shared within these pages. The Scriptures remind us in Hebrews 12:1-2 to "run with patience the race that is set before us, Looking unto Jesus the author and finisher of our faith; who for the joy that was set before him endured the cross, despising the shame, and is set down at the right hand of the throne of God." This foundational truth serves as the bedrock of our journey, anchoring us in the unwavering faithfulness of our Savior as we navigate life's marathon. From the outset, we are called to endurance, recognizing that the Christian life is a marathon, not a sprint, requiring steadfast perseverance and unwavering commitment to the race set before us. Psalm 27:14 echoes this sentiment, encouraging us to "Wait on the Lord: be of good courage, and he shall strengthen thine heart: wait, I say, on the Lord." In moments of trial and tribulation, we are called to patience, trusting in God's timing and provision, "And we know that all things work together for good to them that love God, to them who are the called according to his purpose."(Romans 8:28). Through consistency and selfdiscipline, we strive to live lives that honor God in every thought, word, and deed, knowing that our labor in the Lord is not in vain "Therefore, my beloved brethren, be ye stedfast, unmoveable, always abounding in the work of the Lord, forasmuch as ye know that your labour is not in vain in the Lord. (1 Corinthians 15:58). Galatians 6:9 reminds us to "And let us not be weary in well doing: for in due season we shall reap, if we faint not." With each step forward, we draw upon the resilience and strength that come from our identity in Christ, "I can do all things through Christ which strengtheneth me." (Philippians 4:13). As we navigate the twists and turns of life's journey, we are called to adaptability, recognizing that

God's plans for us are far greater than our own, "For I know the thoughts that I think toward you, saith the Lord, thoughts of peace, and not of evil, to give you an expected end." (Jeremiah 29:11). Proverbs 16:9 reminds us that " A man's heart deviseth his way: but the Lord directeth his steps." In moments of uncertainty, we find solace in the support and encouragement of the community of believers, drawing upon the love and fellowship of the local church to sustain us through life's trials, "And let us consider one another to provoke unto love and to good works: Not forsaking the assembling of ourselves together, as the manner of some is; but exhorting one another: and so much the more, as ye see the day approaching. (Hebrews 10:24-25). And in times of rest and reflection, we find tranquility in the presence of our Savior, who offers rest for our weary souls, "Come unto me, all ye that labour and are heavy laden, and I will give you rest. Take my yoke upon you, and learn of me; for I am meek and lowly in heart: and ye shall find rest unto your souls. For my yoke is easy, and my burden is light. (Matthew 11:28-30). As we stand on the precipice of the next leg of our journey, let us carry these timeless truths with us, ever mindful of the race set before us. With hearts full of hope and hands lifted in praise, let us press on towards the prize, running with endurance and perseverance, knowing that our ultimate goal is to hear the words, "Well done, thou good and faithful servant."

Don't miss out!

Visit the website below and you can sign up to receive emails whenever Joshua Rhoades publishes a new book. There's no charge and no obligation.

https://books2read.com/r/B-A-AJLBB-BUHWE

BOOKS 2 READ

Connecting independent readers to independent writers.

Did you love *The Believer's Pace- Tools for Running Life's Marathon*?
Then you should read *Driven By Faith: Motor Racing Inspired Christian Life*[1] by Joshua Rhoades!

2

"Driven By Faith - Motor Racing Inspired Christian Life" is a captivating fusion of high-speed motor racing and the profound journey of Christian faith. This book accelerates readers into the thrilling world of car racing, drawing powerful parallels between the intricacies of the track and the daily walk of a Christian.Each chapter is meticulously crafted to offer practical Scriptural applications, drawing from the wisdom of the Bible to illuminate the principles of motor racing. Readers will explore how the discipline of maintaining a race car mirrors the spiritual maintenance needed in a Christian's life, with Scriptures highlighting the importance of regular prayer, study, and fellowship.The book considers

---

1. https://books2read.com/u/mlGrP9

2. https://books2read.com/u/mlGrP9

the technicalities of racing, from the precision of pit stops to the strategy of overtaking, illustrating how these elements reflect the Christian virtues of patience, perseverance, and trust in God's timing. Passages like Hebrews 12:1-2 and others, come alive as readers see the race set before them, encouraged to run with endurance and keep their eyes on Jesus, the ultimate champion of faith."Driven By Faith" is rich with detailed insights into the world of motor racing, from the adrenaline of the starting grid to the triumph of the checkered flag. Yet, it is equally rich in spiritual depth, offering readers a roadmap for navigating the twists and turns of life with grace and faith.Whether you're a motorsport enthusiast, a devout Christian, "Driven By Faith - Motor Racing Inspired Christian Life" will fuel your spirit and inspire your soul. Prepare to embark on a journey where faith and racing unite, driving you toward the ultimate finish line with victory in Christ.